D0849834

ARSENAL FC

by Jon Marthaler

SportsZone

EUROPE'S BEST
SOCCER CLUBS

abdopublishing.com

Published by Abdo Publishing, a division of ABDO, PO Box 398166, Minneapolis, Minnesota 55439.
Copyright © 2018 by Abdo Consulting Group, Inc. International copyrights reserved in all countries.
No part of this book may be reproduced in any form without written permission from the publisher.
SportsZone™ is a trademark and logo of Abdo Publishing.

Printed in the United States of America, North Mankato, Minnesota
062017
092017

THIS BOOK CONTAINS
RECYCLED MATERIALS

Cover Photo: BPI/Rex Features/AP Images, foreground; AP Images, background
Interior Photos: Mirrorpix/Newscom, 4, 11; Mealey/Mirrorpix/Newscom, 7; Mark Leech/Mark Leech
Sports Photography/Getty Images, 9, 12; AP Images, 14, 32; Eddie Worth/AP Images, 16; John Walton/
ZumaPress/Newscom, 18; Bob Dear/AP Images, 20; Shutterstock Images, 22, 24, 26; Marc Aspland/
Newscom, 28; Eddie Worth/The Times/News Syndication/AP Images, 30; Keystone Pictures USA/
ZumaPress/Newscom, 34; John Stillwell/Reuters/Newscom, 36; Phil Cole/AllSport/Getty Images Sports/
Getty Images, 38; Jane Mingay/AP Images, 41; John Spencer/Sipa/AP Images, 43

Editor: Patrick Donnelly
Series Designer: Craig Hinton
Content Consultant: Paul Logothetis, European soccer reporter

Publisher's Cataloging-in-Publication Data

Names: Marthaler, Jon, author.
Title: Arsenal FC / by Jon Marthaler.
Description: Minneapolis, MN : Abdo Publishing, 2018. | Series: Europe's best
    soccer clubs | Includes bibliographical references and index.
Identifiers: LCCN 2016962119 | ISBN 9781532111303 (lib. bdg.) |
    ISBN 9781680789157 (ebook)
Subjects: LCSH: Soccer--Europe--History--Juvenile literature. | Soccer teams--
    Europe--History--Juvenile literature. | Soccer--Europe--Records--Juvenile
    literature. | Arsenal Football Club (Soccer team)--Juvenile literature.
Classification: DDC 796.334--dc23
LC record available at http://lccn.loc.gov/2016962119

TABLE OF
CONTENTS

Arsenal forward Alan Smith played a key role in the Miracle at Anfield.

CHAPTER 1

MIRACLE AT ANFIELD

The headline in the British newspaper the *Daily Mirror* on the morning of the game said it all:

"You Haven't Got a Prayer, Arsenal"

It was the final game of the 1988–89 Football League season. Arsenal Football Club (FC) was playing at Liverpool to determine the championship of the top division of English soccer. Liverpool was in first place. Arsenal was in second place. All Liverpool had to do was avoid losing the game by two goals. A win, a tie, or even a one-goal loss would give Liverpool the title.

EUROPEAN SOCCER

The European soccer season is broken down into different levels of competition. It can be confusing to keep track of it all. Here's a handy guide to help you follow the action.

League Play

The 20 best teams in England play in the Premier League. Teams play all league opponents twice each season for 38 total games. The three teams with the worst records are relegated—or sent down—to the second division, which sends three teams up to replace them the next season. The Premier League debuted in 1992–93. It replaced the Football League First Division (1888–1991) as England's top league.

European Play

The top four teams in the Premier League qualify for the Union of European Football Associations (UEFA) Champions League. This annual tournament involves the best teams from the top leagues throughout Europe. The Champions League started in 1992. It replaced the European Cup, a similar tournament that began in 1955.

The next three teams in the Premier League qualify for the UEFA Europa League. The Europa League is Europe's second-tier tournament. It runs in a similar manner to the Champions League but crowns its own winner. The Europa League debuted in 1971 as the UEFA Cup but was renamed in 2009.

Domestic Cups

Almost every English team from any level of competition is eligible to play for the Football Association Challenge Cup (FA Cup). The tournament typically includes several hundred teams, including the professional teams from the Premier League. Founded in 1871–72, the FA Cup is the oldest soccer tournament in the world. The League Cup is a similar tournament. It involves teams from only the top four divisions in England.

Michael Thomas reacts to the action on the field at Anfield.

Liverpool was the best team in English soccer. It won 10 championships in 16 seasons between 1973 and 1988. Arsenal had not won at Anfield, Liverpool's stadium, in almost 15 years.

Beating Liverpool at Anfield that day seemed almost impossible. Winning by two goals was even less likely.

It had been an uneven season for Arsenal. The team known as the Gunners was in first place at Christmas and stayed there almost the rest of the year. But they stumbled in the season's final weeks. Meanwhile, Liverpool put together a 24-game unbeaten streak to pass Arsenal in the standings, setting the stage for the final-day showdown.

Scoreless Start

Neither team scored in the first half. Steve Bould had a decent chance for Arsenal, but his header in the box was deflected away by a Liverpool defender. With just 45 minutes left, Arsenal still had to score twice and keep Liverpool off the board.

Arsenal earned a free kick early in the second half. The ball was 35 yards (32 m) from Liverpool's goal. Nigel Winterburn lofted it toward the back post of the net. Arsenal forward Alan Smith charged around the Liverpool defense and got behind his defender. He slightly touched the ball with his head and the ball bounced into the net. Arsenal led

Liverpool's John Aldridge, left, and Arsenal's Steve Bould contest a header.

1–0. Forty minutes remained in the game. But Arsenal needed another goal.

Forward Michael Thomas got a good chance in the 74th minute. He had the ball in front of the goal. But he couldn't get much speed on his shot. It went straight to the Liverpool goalkeeper. Arsenal fans thought the team had missed its best chance to score again. Surely Liverpool's defense would shut things down from there.

Just in Time

The clock reached 90 minutes. Arsenal still led 1–0. All that remained was injury time. The referee could blow his whistle to end the game at any second. Liverpool midfielder Steve McMahon held up one finger. He screamed to his teammates, "One minute to go!" Liverpool practically had another trophy in hand.

Arsenal's Lee Dixon got the ball in his own half. He lofted it down the field. Smith collected the ball. He chipped a pass forward to Thomas. The ball bounced wildly between Thomas's leg and a Liverpool defender. Suddenly it bounced free, leaving Thomas wide open in front of the goal!

Exhausted Liverpool players can't hide their disappointment after Michael Thomas scored his game-winning goal.

Thomas steadied himself. The goalkeeper came out to stop him. But he dove to his right as Thomas flicked the ball the opposite way into the back corner of the net.

From left, Tony Adams, Steve Bould, and David O'Leary celebrate Arsenal's stunning victory at Anfield in 1989.

Thomas did a somersault in celebration in the penalty area. Arsenal's players and fans went crazy. The Gunners led by two goals, exactly what they needed to win the title.

Within a minute, the referee blew his whistle and the game was over. Arsenal had not won a title in 18 years. Liverpool had won 10 in that time. But this time Arsenal was the Football League champion.

A banner hangs in Arsenal's stadium that reads "ANFIELD '89." It's a reminder of that amazing night. It's a reminder of that impossible win. It's a reminder of Michael Thomas's last-second heroics for a club that wouldn't quit.

CHAPTER 2

WOOLWICH TO WENGER

Arsenal might not be the best team in English history, but it's been more consistent than anyone. Arsenal has been in England's first division since 1919. During that time, every other team in England has spent at least one season out of the first division. Arsenal's streak is the longest in the country. And the whole thing started with a munitions factory.

In 1886, the only professional soccer teams in England were in the northern part of the country. In London, which is in the south, all of the teams were amateur teams. There was no organized Football League. The Football League wouldn't kick

Arsenal and Stoke square off in a 1937 match at Highbury.

off until 1889. There was no World Cup. The only international tournament was between teams from the British Isles: England, Ireland, Scotland, and Wales.

Royal Arsenal Football Club was founded in December 1886. The club members were men who worked at the Arsenal munitions factory in Woolwich, in southeast London. The club played there for 20 years. However, transportation options were somewhat limited in that part of the city. As a result, the team struggled to draw fans. Something had to change.

Changing Places

In 1913 Arsenal moved to north London. Its new stadium was called Highbury after the neighborhood where the stadium was located. The stadium was just two blocks from the Gillespie Road station on the London Underground. That made it easy for fans to get to the games on the train. The club also renamed itself from Royal Arsenal FC to Arsenal FC.

FAST FACT

Arsenal rented Highbury from St. John's College of Divinity until 1925. As part of the lease agreement, the club had to agree not to stage games on Good Friday and Christmas Day.

In 1925, the club hired Herbert Chapman as manager. He turned Arsenal into a successful club. Chapman's changes led

Fans sit next to the statue of Herbert Chapman outside Emirates Stadium, Arsenal's current home.

to five Football League championships and two FA Cup titles in eight years. He was a genius at finding players that fit his system perfectly. He changed Arsenal's formation so that there were more players in the midfield and defense. But the players were also better at quickly attacking and scored lots of goals. Chapman died in 1934, but the team he built kept winning.

Double Glory in 1971

The Gunners won the league championship in 1948 and 1953. But they struggled for many years afterward. The exception was in 1970–71. Arsenal needed a win or a scoreless draw in the season's final game to win the Football League title. The game happened to be at Tottenham Hotspur, Arsenal's biggest rival. So many fans showed up that the stadium was full and the gates were locked an hour before the game started. Arsenal's Ray Kennedy scored the only goal of the game in the 87th minute. It gave the team its first trophy in 18 years.

Less than a week later, the team took home its second trophy of the season. Arsenal met Liverpool in the FA Cup Final.

FAST FACT
The London Underground, or Tube, is a system of subway trains in London. Chapman convinced the authorities to rename Gillespie Road station Arsenal station. It is still the only Tube station named after a sports team.

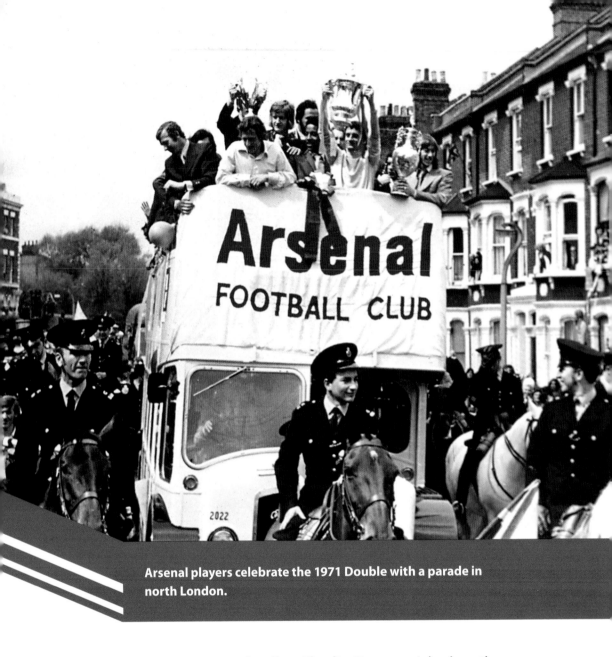

Arsenal players celebrate the 1971 Double with a parade in north London.

Late in extra time, Arsenal striker Charlie George picked up the ball 25 yards (23 m) from Liverpool's goal. He rocketed a shot into the top corner. Arsenal held on for the 2–1 win. It gave the team its first Double—or two trophies in one season, in this case the league title and the FA Cup—in its history.

Graham's Gunners, Arsène's Arsenal

In 1986, George Graham took over as manager. He started Arsenal on the path to glory. A League Cup win in 1987 was a sign of good things to come. Winning the league title at Anfield in 1989 was a big step. But Arsenal's 1991 team might have been even better. It lost only one game all season and won the title. The Gunners also won the Cup Double (FA Cup and League Cup) in 1993.

Another change in 1996 would affect the club's future for the next two decades, though few realized it at the time. A little-known French coach named Arsène Wenger was hired as the club's manager that year. Wenger went on to reinvent the club. Before Wenger, Arsenal was a good team but not a great one. Wenger turned it into one of the best teams in Europe.

Wenger's Arsenal teams played a free-flowing exciting style. Superstars like forward Thierry Henry proved to be a perfect fit. The Gunners also became a threat to win trophies every season.

The Gunners moved into their new state-of-the-art Emirates Stadium in 2006.

Under Wenger, Arsenal won the Double in both 1998 and 2002, setting the stage for a remarkable feat. Arsenal went the entire 2003–04 league season without a loss. It was the first team to do so since Preston North End 115 years earlier. Besides those triumphs, Wenger's team also won the FA Cup four times through 2016.

Wenger's success also set the club up for a new era. Because of the money his teams brought in, the club could afford to build a new, bigger stadium. At the end of the 2005–06 season, Arsenal moved from Highbury two blocks down the road to Emirates Stadium. Highbury was converted into apartments by the team and sold.

FAST FACT

Wenger was still Arsenal's manager in 2017. That made him the longest-tenured manager in European soccer.

Arsenal finished in fourth place or better in each of Wenger's first 20 seasons. The team also made it to the final 16 of the Champions League in every season from 2001 to 2016. That streak was snapped in the 2016–17 season when Arsenal finished in fifth place, one point out of the top four. However, the Gunners salvaged the season with a 2–1 victory over league champion Chelsea in the FA Cup Final. That gave Arsenal its third FA Cup title in the past four seasons.

CHAPTER 3

The club's crest pays tribute to its origins in a munitions factory.

THE GUNNERS

Arsenal's Latin motto is *Victoria Concordia Crescit*. Translated, it means "Victory grows out of harmony." Another way of saying this is "moving forward together."

The motto is just one of many traditions that define the club. For example, Arsenal always decorates the Emirates Stadium directors box with flowers in the colors of the opposing team. That simple act displays the sportsmanship and fair play expected throughout the club ranks.

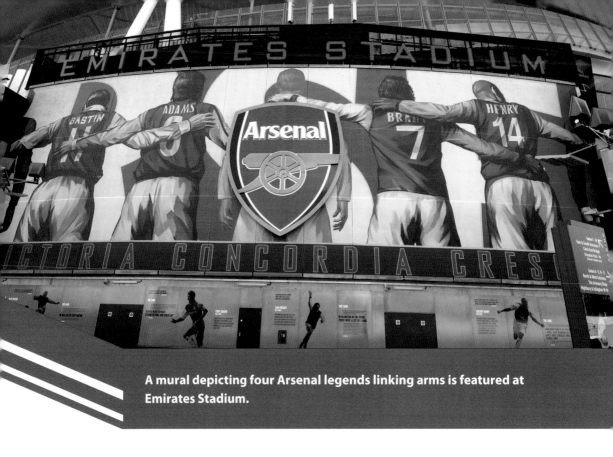

A mural depicting four Arsenal legends linking arms is featured at Emirates Stadium.

Looking Good

Arsenal players wear red jerseys with white sleeves. Originally the team wore all red. Manager Herbert Chapman is said to have spotted a man wearing a red sleeveless sweater over a white shirt in 1933. It inspired him to create a new jersey. The team's home jersey has been the same ever since.

Big Rivals

Since the team moved to north London in 1913, it has had a fierce rivalry with Tottenham Hotspur. Tottenham also is located in North London. Its fans weren't happy that Arsenal moved into the neighborhood. The North London Derby is one of the biggest rivalries in England. Arsenal has had the upper hand for most of the past 50 years. Its fans love to celebrate "St. Totteringham's Day." This is the day when the Spurs can no longer catch Arsenal in the standings. Tottenham had finished behind Arsenal for 21 consecutive seasons before finally snapping the streak in 2016–17.

An Incredible Season

Arsenal can also claim the best league season in English soccer history. The Gunners went through the entire 2003–04 Premier League season without losing a game. They won 26 games and had 12 draws. It was the first time since 1888–89 that a team had gone undefeated. In 1888–89 Preston North End had

18 wins and four draws in 22 games. Arsenal had to go 38 games unbeaten to match that record. That team is known as the "Invincibles." It ended up with a 49-game unbeaten streak overall. That was also a record.

Under manager Arsène Wenger, the team has been fun to watch. Wenger's preferred method of attack is through many short passes instead of a few longer passes. When Wenger arrived in 1996, Arsenal had a reputation for being boring. The team won a lot of games 1–0. In fact, fans would sing a song called "One-nil to the Arsenal," to reflect that common final score. But Wenger's teams scored a lot. It seemed like they were playing a totally different sport.

Arsenal and Tottenham Hotspur square off at least twice each season in the North London Derby.

CHAPTER 4

STARS OF THE PAST

Arsenal had a strong run in the 1930s, led by the team's first big stars. Many teams played with four forwards and three midfielders. Manager Herbert Chapman moved a forward back to the midfield to help control the ball. This key player was Scottish midfielder Alex James. He was the center of the team's offense. James did not score very much, but his passing was legendary.

Cliff Bastin played left wing on those teams. On other teams, the left wing would stay wide. Bastin liked to cut in toward the

Ted Drake falls forward after taking a shot against Sheffield United in the 1936 FA Cup Final at Wembley Stadium.

middle of the field to get in position to score. Bastin scored 178 goals for Arsenal. That was the club record from 1938 until 1997.

Two men played forward alongside James on those teams. David Jack played from 1928 to 1934. His biggest year was the 1930–31 season, when he scored 34 goals. He scored in nine straight games that year. That remained a club record through 2016.

Ted Drake took over when Jack retired and played until 1939. Drake had his own impressive feat in 1934–35, his first year in the starting lineup. He scored 44 goals, 42 of them in league play. Both marks are still club records. In a 7–1 win against Aston Villa the next season, Drake scored all seven Arsenal goals. Overall, Drake scored 139 goals for Arsenal, while Jack scored 124.

The 1971 Double

Frank McLintock was the club captain for many years. He played center back for the 1971 team that won the Double. McLintock was named the Footballer of the Year that season as the league's best player. Midfielder George Graham also was a key player for that 1971 team. He was a stylish force in the center of the field. His relaxed style earned him the nickname "Stroller." He played completely unhurried. But he also scored a lot of important goals for the team.

Fans swarm Arsenal captain Frank McLintock as he shows off the FA Cup trophy at a team celebration in 1971.

The most important player on that 1970–71 team was Charlie George. Usually a forward, George played as an attacking midfielder that year. It gave him a chance to drive the entire team's attack forward. His most famous goal was the game-winner against Liverpool in the 1971 FA Cup Final.

1989, 1991, and Beyond

Arsenal was famous for its defense in the late 1980s and 1990s. Center back Tony Adams was the leader. Adams was the club captain for 14 years. His career included four league championships, three FA Cup titles, and two League Cups. A statue of Adams stands outside the North Bank at Emirates Stadium. It shows him with his arms spread wide after scoring the final goal in a 4–0 win over Everton to clinch the 1998 Premier League championship.

Goalkeeper David Seaman was equally important to the team. Many people thought he was the best keeper in the world when he joined Arsenal in 1990. He was a big reason that Arsenal allowed just 18 goals in the entire 1990–91 season.

Ian Wright joined Arsenal in 1991. He helped the team become known for something besides defense. He led the league in scoring in his first season. This included a hat trick in the final game of the year. Wright retired with 185 goals for Arsenal. It was the club record at the time.

Arsène Wenger, *left*, holds the league trophy while captain Tony Adams hoists the FA Cup after Arsenal won its Double in 2002.

Between 1985 and 1992, the Arsenal fans' favorite player might have been David "Rocky" Rocastle. He won two League titles as a central midfielder. He was both fast and strong, and he never quit. Sadly, he died from cancer in 2001, just two years after he retired. To celebrate him, Arsenal fans hung a "Rocky" banner in the stadium. It hangs permanently at Emirates Stadium. At almost any Arsenal game today, you'll still hear fans sing "Oh Rocky Rocky." It often comes in the seventh minute, because Rocastle wore the No. 7 jersey.

CHAPTER 5

Arsène Wenger, right, changed the culture throughout England by signing foreign stars such as Thierry Henry, left.

MODERN STARS

Arsène Wenger changed not only Arsenal but all of English soccer when he took over as manager in 1996. Before Wenger, most of the league's players were from Great Britain. Wenger brought in players from all of Europe. His teams favored a stylish passing game. English teams at the time favored kicking long balls forward to strikers. Wenger wanted to create offense through passing.

British Foundations, Foreign Flair

Wenger first built teams using the British core of the 1980s. The 1998 Double winners featured David Seaman, the famous Back Four, and Ian Wright. But the team also included standout foreign players. Dutch forward Dennis Bergkamp and winger Marc Overmars led the scoring. Patrick Vieira and Emmanuel Petit of France ran the midfield. French striker Nicolas Anelka came off the bench.

The Invincibles

By 2003–04, most of the Arsenal roster came from outside England. In its final game, Arsenal beat Leicester City 2–1 to clinch an undefeated season. Only two of Arsenal's starting 11 were English. Players from Brazil, Sweden, the Ivory Coast, and Cameroon also were on the field.

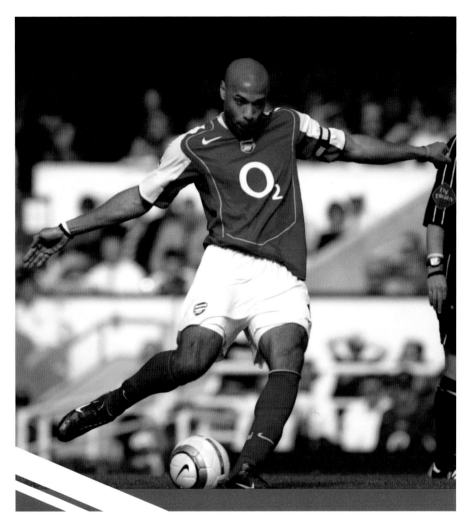

Thierry Henry was voted by Arsenal fans as the greatest player in club history.

Bergkamp set up both Arsenal goals. Vieira scored one. French striker Thierry Henry scored the other on a penalty kick. Henry's goal-scoring ability, Bergkamp's passing, Robert Pirès's creativity, and Vieira's power were key for Arsenal. They represented the high point of the Wenger era.

Henry arrived at Arsenal in 1999 after playing for Monaco in France's top league and with Italian club Juventus. When he joined Arsenal, Wenger converted him from a winger to a center forward. The move worked out better than he could have hoped. Henry led the Premier League in scoring four times and was named the league Player of the Year three times. He was known for his speed, his power, his ability to dribble through defenses, and his precision shooting. More than any other player, Henry was the perfect example of Wenger's Arsenal—beautiful to watch, relentless, and a goal-scorer of the highest order. The club honored him with a statue outside of Emirates Stadium.

Today's Arsenal

The Premier League is popular all over the world. It is no longer notable for foreign players to succeed in England. Every team has big-name imports, not just Arsenal. These days, it's still a mix of locals and internationals that lead the Arsenal team.

Chilean striker Alexis Sanchez has been one of Arsenal's best scorers. Short and powerful, he led Arsenal in goals in 2014–15. Many of those goals came off passes from German winger Mesüt Özil. English winger Theo Walcott also scores plenty of

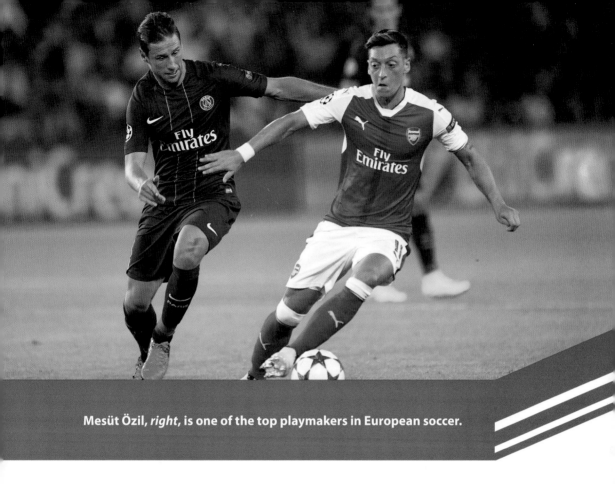

Mesüt Özil, *right*, is one of the top playmakers in European soccer.

goals off Özil's passes. Frenchman Laurent Koscielny, Germans Per Mertesacker and Shkodran Mustafi, and Spain's Hector Bellerin lead the team's defense.

In 2006, Arsenal moved to Emirates Stadium. For several years afterward, the club's debts made it hard for them to compete with the richest teams in the league. Today, the club has plenty of money to spend. FA Cup wins in 2014, 2015, and 2017 show that the club is once again ready to challenge the best teams in Europe.

ARSENAL FC
TEAM FILE

NAME: Arsenal Football Club

YEAR FORMED: 1886

WHERE THEY PLAY: Emirates Stadium, London, England

LEAGUE TITLES: 13 (the most recent in 2003–04)

FA CUPS: 13 (the most recent in 2017)

LEAGUE CUPS: 2 (1988, 1993)

KEY RECORDS

- Went undefeated in the Premier League in 2003–04, the only team to do so since 1889

- Has been in the top division since 1919, the longest streak in England.

- Was undefeated for 49 consecutive league matches, the longest streak in English league history

AUTHOR'S DREAM TEAM

GOALKEEPER: David Seaman

DEFENSE: Lee Dixon, Tony Adams, Steve Bould, Nigel Winterburn

MIDFIELD: Robert Pirés, Patrick Vieira, Liam Brady, Cliff Bastin

FORWARDS: Thierry Henry, Dennis Bergkamp

TIMELINE

1886

Royal Arsenal Football Club is founded in southeast London by men who work at the Woolwich Arsenal ammunition factory.

1930

Arsenal wins its first FA Cup.

1931

Arsenal wins the Football League for the first time, one of its five titles in the 1930s.

1971

Arsenal wins both the Football League and the FA Cup, the team's first Double.

1989

Arsenal wins the Football League on the last day, beating Liverpool 2–0 with a goal in injury time to clinch the trophy.

1996

Manager Arsène Wenger is hired and becomes the man most responsible for building the modern-day Arsenal.

2002

Arsenal wins its third Double and its second in five years, having accomplished the feat in 1998.

2004

Arsenal's "Invincibles" go an entire Premier League season undefeated, the first team to do so in the English first division since 1889.

2006

Arsenal moves out of Highbury, its home since 1913, and into the new Emirates Stadium, just two blocks away.

2015

Arsenal wins its second consecutive FA Cup title and 12th overall.

GLOSSARY

center back

A defender who plays in the middle of the field.

derby

An ongoing competition between two teams from the same region or city.

extra time

Two 15-minute periods added to a game if the score is tied at the end of regulation.

forward

Also called a striker, the player who plays nearest the opponent's goal.

free kick

An unguarded kick awarded to a team after a foul.

hat trick

Three goals by the same player in one game.

injury time

Also called stoppage time, the time added at the end of each half to account for injuries and other stoppages.

midfielder

A player who stays mostly in the middle third of the field and links the defenders with the forwards.

munitions factory

A factory where weapons and ammunition are made.

winger

An attacking midfielder who plays wide.

FOR MORE INFORMATION

BOOKS

Marthaler, Jon. *Soccer Trivia*. Minneapolis, MN: Abdo Publishing, 2016.

McDougall, Chrös. *Best Sport Ever: Soccer*. Minneapolis, MN: Abdo Publishing, 2012.

Monnig, Alex. *The World Cup*. Minneapolis, MN: Abdo Publishing, 2013.

WEBSITES

To learn more about Arsenal, visit abdobooklinks.com. These links are routinely monitored and updated to provide the most current information available.

PLACE TO VISIT

EMIRATES STADIUM
Hornsey Rd, London N7 7AJ, United Kingdom
Phone: +44 20 7619 5003
bookings.arsenal.com/stadiumtours

Watching a game in person is fun, but even on off days, fans can tour the stadium and visit the Arsenal Museum. The self-guided audio tour includes visits to the director's box, the home and visiting locker rooms, and the media facilities, as well as a chance to stand on the field. The tour includes admission to the Arsenal museum, which is full of artifacts and history that date back to the club's founding.

INDEX

ABOUT THE AUTHOR

Jon Marthaler has been a freelance sportswriter for more than 10 years. He writes a weekly soccer column for the *Minneapolis Star Tribune*. He lives in St. Paul, Minnesota, with his wife and daughter.